This Passage

POEMS

BY

CAROL L. DEERING

SASTRUGI PRESS

JACKSON, WY

For permission requests, write to the publisher, addressed:
Attention: Permissions Coordinator
Sastrugi Press, P.O. Box 1297, Jackson, WY 83001, United States.
www.sastrugipress.com

This is a work of poetry. Some parts have been fictionalized in varying
degrees, for various purposes. Some names and identifying details of people
and locations described in this work may have been altered to protect their
privacy.

Library of Congress Cataloging-in-Publication Data
Names: Deering, Carol L.
Title: This Passage : poems / 1st United States Edition
p. cm.
1. Deering, Andy J. (1947-2020). 2. Poetry, American. 3. Poliomyelitis. 4.
Disabilities—Poetry. 5. Grief—Poetry.
Identifiers: LCCN 2024040339 | ISBN 9781649223548 (paperback)
LC record available at https://lccn.loc.gov/2024040339
Summary: The poems in this collection by Carol L. Deering reflect the reali-
ties of struggle, strength, and love as she and her late husband (who contract-
ed polio) live through waves of happiness, creativity, a sense of humor ~ and
the increasing urgency of disabilities. His passing and her survivor's grief lead
through sorrow and approach a journey of healing.

ISBN-13: 978-1-64922-354-8 (Paperback)

PS3604.E44 T4 2024
811.6 Dee

Cover image © 2024 Carol L. Deering (author)

Interior design by Kelly's Book Layout, kellygaffney232@gmail.com
00215
10 9 8 7 6 5 4 3 2

"Carol Deering has captured both the pain and beauty of human suffering in her exquisite collection of poetry. My life includes a similar journey as I contracted a rare form of West Nile poliomyelitis. Reading her poems brings back memories of feeling invisible, and held captive by a wheelchair. The thoughts and feelings of living with such uncertainty. These poems take you deep into those emotions and will resonate at some level with all humanity."

—**Lynne McAuliffe**, Dean of Business, Technical, Health & Safety, Central Wyoming College.

"This is the most powerful and personal collection of poetry I have ever read! It is a marvel that does not dabble in sappiness, but reveals a heart torn by loss but thrilled by love and memory—a tour de force in the choice of precise details to carry the emotional weight."

—**Tom Spence**, author of *Observations and Commentary: One Hundred Poems*

"I'm not much of a connoisseur of poetry, but I liked this. It was interesting to see the health problems slowly add up over the years, subtly in the background, while describing his interest in other things like animals, music, motorcycles. As a doctor, I tended to focus on bacteria, breathing, and injuries. It was enlightening to see a different perspective."

—**John Reckling**, M.D.

"This poetry book is a rite of passage: a long marriage, disabilities, death, grief, and return. It is a book for those of an age, those immersed in our human condition. Deering is a poet of sensitivity, and selectivity; she brings a longing and leaning into nature as a kind of contrapuntal music to the decline of her husband, Andy. '…a hush of lake…' 'rain-damp trees' 'you can't swallow…' 'a morning frayed to rags.' The poet endeavors to remember and keep, but also to let go into art. All of nature is bringing joy; but the nature of the body of Andy brings pain. The labor of the author to support while 'you doze off in mid-sentence' and then, his death. In the poem Utter Loneliness, the form is broken, and 'the day's back/is turned to me.' And yet, at the end of the book, the poet declares in the section A Splash of Sun: 'Tenderness/ speaks to us//of fleeting certainty.' A book of our time."

—**Veronica Golos**, author of *GIRL* (winner, International Naji Naaman Honor Prize for Poetry, Beirut, Lebanon), and *Vocabulary of Silence* (winner, New Mexico Poetry Award).

"This is a masterful collection of feelings, emotions, and words!"

—**Echo Klaproth**, former Wyoming Poet Laureate, Hospice Chaplain, and author of *A Requiem to the Vitality of Life*.

CONTENTS

PREFACE

These poems are about Andy Deering, my husband of 45 years. Poetry is the best way I can tell his story, though it's impossible to tell it all. He had a great sense of humor and curiosity. He was young in spirit, read for pleasure, loved animals, writing, as well as music, art, Native cultures, motorcycles, libraries, teaching, human and animal rights – and stood for their value, even when he couldn't stand.

Andy died near the beginning of covid, but not of covid. He'd been struggling with the effects of another virus: the poliovirus, which he contracted at one year old. He'd been fortunate to undergo a controversial treatment pioneered by Sister Kenny, an Australian nurse who advocated a hot-water-and-blanket compress which calmed the children's muscle spasms. Still, the virus lurked.

At five, Andy moved with his parents to Arizona, in hopes that the dry climate would help with his asthma attacks. He wore an ankle brace, then used a walking stick, or a crutch and cane, to help his balance. He was fitted for a leg brace, and used it to walk and eventually stand up from an electric scooter. Two progressively more substantial wheelchairs followed. Days before he died, we learned he'd been approved for a new-style wheelchair that would have let him sit higher and not be overlooked in a crowd.

Everyone's grief is different, but there's a space in our hearts that draws us together. When they wheeled that zippered bag down the ramp, I honestly wondered, 'Why am I still breathing?' We were so close for so many years, I couldn't make sense of a life without him!

I had the feeling 'I am nowhere, now.' Times were hard, with 'strangled choices from computer voices … synching data to a cloud.' No one wanted to hear loneliness.

Some days, I cry from an unexpected kindness that still exists in the world. And the sparkle I can't ignore: a sense that Andy is sometimes near. Every day of our togetherness was real life. I never thought I'd be writing a book about him! But working on these poems has helped me get through some rough patches.

I hope they help *you*, too.

I. POSSIBILITIES

We pinned our hopes
on youth, togetherness,

wild continuance…

THIS PASSAGE

Gardens nod to breeze or storm, volcanic ash.
Lightning chases dusk through the trees.
A roof parts the rain as we lay entangled,
listening to water let down her hair.

The trucks and tents we camped in.
The sunflower backroads we trolled.
Our landlady shooing plump sheep
from her overgrown gladiolas.
The Power of Love in full bloom.

Pain cleared its throat like a whip: Cane/Crutch/Brace/
Inhaler./Clumsy rolling chair./A ramp creaking
wooden to our door. Shadows burnt, bled, macabre.
Bleak bright shades of Edward Hopper.
Your mom, scrubbing her kitchen in hymns...

But we held fast to reading, wildlife, art
and friendships, a soft tomato rain.
And, dreamily, to a family!
Whatever sparkle we could bring.

A buck, struggling with his heavy crown,
bows slightly, thrown off pace. The lead doe
turns her face full 'round. And, one ear to the side,
accommodates her stride.

All our stories spun and polished by the wind.
The valiant swath we made *as we passed through...*

MONSOON

You were a mountain when we met.
I was stumbling rivers
      running incoherent
in a storm two thousand miles
from home. Crack, Rumble. Boom!

Monsoon, they called it.
Hair, clothes,
      I dripped distress
through all the side streets of confidence,
my first day on the job.

      I shivered drizzly stupor.
          You soaked up every drop.

You kept arriving early. Mystery,
accomplishment. Passion
      for music, books, rhinoceri.
Chamisa charming butterflies.
The Western meadowlark song.

You spoke of your slight limp,
crippled arm, problematic breathing.
      I was drawn
to your sense of humor, energy,
your large-as-living smile…

MOONLIGHT SWEET AS BAKLAVA

We were that light,
that far outside the laws of gravity.
Nothing could touch us.
                                  ~ Danusha Laméris

You were engaged when we met, and you chose
            to honor that. And by some quirky
twist of fate, I stood up for your fiancée.
            Weddings. Divorces ~ mine on Valentine's.

            Unexpected storylines

                    flipped

and carnivaled, waking a fresh sunrise.

Bright skies, icicles. Snow
            plunging from a sun-roused pine
like a Steller's jay to an opened cone.

We lazed in pinyon-juniper, the sun,
            slow pocket watch, winding down.

Chanced upon obsidian, as twilight
            tucked the gibbous moon
into a hush of lake.

And, buoyed by the soft-fallen dusk, stretched
            the time it could take

            to float back from a kiss...

CAGED

Morning in the rain-damp trees.
Look up, a twig-basket sky!

      You fall in our rented home,
      your tougher ankle sprained.

Sun grates on its hinges. Angled winds
ride herd on last year's leaves.

      You, whisked in an ambulance.
      X-rays. Two weeks you cannot walk.

Flash of the future! Storms tripping over
their intermittent clouds.

      Your fingers flap a harmonica,
      wing of an injured bird.

A warm breeze starts lapping, ruffling
the trees like tall puppies.

      You read. I play comedienne,
      caregiver, courier to your staff.

Library week, a fifth-grader
presents a garter snake in a cage. You laugh.

      You're on the mend! I pretend
      you'll dance with me some day...

STEP INTO A GEODE

Sure, you'd fall at times, but you had a grace
about you, a light that changed November leaves
from drab to ruby. *A laugh inciting spring.*

All those surgeries as a child. Muscles swapped
like puzzle pieces. You learned to walk
three times. *But you could never jump or run.*

Polio grounded you. Wind clawed the clouds to
ribbon-candy, played solitaire with the leaves.
You'd spend recess with insects, plants,
inscrutable stones, spotting
      birds that others never saw or heard.

You grew in music. Choir, men's glee. Easter sunrise
on the South Rim. Cornet in the concert band.
A soldier in South Pacific. *But you could never march.*

A cat-scratch inflated your arm. Asthma gripped you.
Fragrances, dust. New-mown grass or hay. You'd fall
like a slip from a hanger. *Your left arm had to raise your right.*

But you could step into a geode,
sliced by a diamond saw,
a classroom dark with jewels,
      sit anywhere, and you'd glow!

HELPING SNAKES ACROSS THE ROAD

All confidence, you'd stop the car
      on a mountain road, emerge
with your walking stick, and nudge
      a sleepy snake, dressed in its gown
of elegant scales, escorting it
      like a lover, across the road, away
from cars or trucks
      which might not choose to stop.

Once, by acres of smooth desert sand,
      you swung your door so I could see
a sidewinder's sinuous wriggles
      as it slid away. A melody of curvature,
scrawled just for us, and the waning,
      self-satisfied sun.

You majored in biology, wishing to be
      a ranger walking forests' mud or
rocky trails, taming rowdy fires. But
      your weak leg and risky breathing
dampened those desires.

So you shared all the knowledge you
      gained in college, leaving in cap
and gown, to nudge the rest of us
      across the threshold of our fears.

A LOVELINESS

Low clouds,
the Grand Canyon,
a cool forgiving mist.
Heightened scent
of rain. Vitality
we gulped and

celebrated.

Evergreen trunks
dressed in ladybugs,
masses of ladybugs,
like a coarse-knit
blood-wine shawl,
red dwarf stars

in frenzy.

We pinned our hopes
on youth, togetherness,
wild continuance.
A loveliness
of ladybugs
head-over-heels

on the rim.

LA JOLLA WEEKEND

In this photo, you're standing
by the scraggly tracks of tidepools
etched in rock, the sea aloof, wringing,
pressing her lacy lingerie.

A pool rich with dark anemones,
shadowy trickery, engages you.

> *You moved unsteadily*
> *with your walking stick, around*
> *but not between   the holes.*

Boulders caked with prickly lichen
sport cavities, tiny nodes. A footlong
slate, bristling with blue mussels, seaweed
by its side, piques our appetite.

The taste of salt jumping on our tongues!

> *I took the pictures. You'd spout*
> *biology, spawned from memory.*
> *No way to write that down…*

Moment to moment, wave
                jostling wave.

> *No way to ask you   now.*

ONE HEARTBEAT IN A BLAZE

Could it be the detectives? Sherlock with his cherrywood
pipe? Bogart's tough-guy cigarette stance? Columbo,
who thought better with a lit cigar?

You were intrigued by the bookstore humidor,
its sweet array of smells. The loopy meander
of a smoke ring, a match in the ashtray
departing like a blaze-colored sail.

Once in Canada, you bought a pack of Sweet Caporal,
tore the paper and changed the spelling,
Caporal to Carol. I carried that scrap in my wallet
for years.

I worried about your left lung, never fully developed.
The surgeon general's warning on every pack.
And we'd argue.

One brisk October night, smoking at the wheel,
you tell me: *No, this smoke is Not hurting
your eyes!* and *No, you do Not need to lower your window,
even an inch!* What?!

We're each of us a flash of lightning, a puff of smoke,
a wavering musical note, in and out of this body,
this galaxy, as we rest and ponder the fear and wonder
of our next blaze...

THE RISING SLUSH

We slogged in a freakish blizzard
across that parking lot. You held onto me
nonstop, through the rising slush.

> *The break-in! Our new amp, speakers,*
> *stereo ~ no more! Cow manure*
> *smeared the shared washer.*
> *Frozen fish, loud as cowboy boots,*
> *hushed as the dryer thawed.*
> *Huge motorcycles lording over all.*

Trying to rush without rushing.
The wet paper sack undressing
all our groceries for the week.
Just as we reached the patio, swoosh!
You did the splits, dragging me slowly down.

> *The manager kept a meat cleaver*
> *and a long-blade combat knife*
> *inside his door, and froze*
> *when he heard my steps*
> *climbing to pay the rent.*

Three weeks more and we could move.
No tubular bells clang-chiming the nights!.
No brutal fights above!

> *Hope coaxed a sluggish river, icing over*
> *against the pull of its wings,*
> *to carry us out to the countryside,*
> *where we could grow sweet dreams…*

SULLEN ROSES: MAY 18, 1980

I heard it while weeding
our hen-pecked garden.
A perfect white-cone dragon
spewed after weeks of drunken
grumbling. An inner seething
held no more. Just another boom,
you thought. We rode the cycle
to our friends'. Sat stirring cream
in coffee, friendship lazy,
the light softening…

Their TV never once declared emergency.

Seagulls bolted west, then flurried
back. Sullen roses dimmed the sky
then burst as dismal ash. Our inner
soothing held no more. Streetlights,
caught napping, roused at noon.

Homeward, you blasted slithery roads,
helmets housing our fears. All night
you struggled breathing. Dust, hay.
Now ash, debris.

Morning, a plaintive cheep, repeating.
Bird in need of a reply…

~ *for Bob & Sandra*

SPRAY

What is all this juice and all this joy?
~ Gerard Manley Hopkins

Gamecocks crow, rip flowers.
Sun sparks and dazzles. The brio
of Spanish words and laughter

music from the orchard trees.

The pollen hassles you. Fear
slips through me, like a cold gust
through a stand of poplars.

You can't swallow your allergy pills!

Cherries stored, the braceros leave.
You head inside for your inhaler.
Cropdusters begin to spray.

I pluck our sheets from the line.

LOST & LOOKING FOR FULTON CANYON

You'd been driving all the narrow curvy roads,
the morning frayed to rags.

Whose idea was this? Surely, it was mine.
In the silence, I ponder what I know.

> *You had double-pneumonia, polio*
> *as a child. Now allergies: pollen,*
> *sulfa, penicillin…*

The road swirls its dust, pings its tiny stones,
then gulps the icy puddles we smash.
I fidget and recall.

> *Your gall bladder, just removed.*
> *A cyst on your back. A new drug*
> *painting a dark splotchy rash…*

Wearily you say:
> *Look. I can't make it for you out of thin air!*

Innocently I say:
> *Isn't that what canyons are made of?*

You swivel your head to dodge my eyes,
then double back with a silly grin.

GLORY DAYS

Your eyes pursued the curves,
your body careening, presiding
over the road. The breeze
so alive, the mist from a field
surprising. Horsepower at the flip
of a wrist. You and your motorcycle
on a quest. Unquenchable desire.

Skipping classes, tracking shortcuts
to the wild. Inhaling the scent of shredding
sycamore, rattling their spiky seedballs,
tossing their winged pips like accidents
to the ground. Roaming farther, free as fire…

You were a surfer on Mt. Lemmon,
reading the spiral waves, leaning forward,
veering wide, into the rush of day.
I clasped your waist, then tugged
your shirt, so I wouldn't face the blast
alone.

Back in town, 108°, another cycle
roared in front, a bag of frozen cubes
bungeed to its rack. The thrill of icy splash!

Time passed. Your knees and muscles
kept releasing you, to the floor, the steps,
the road. The Yamaha rested in our shed
for years. Mice built a nest in the tailpipe.
You never rode again. The wrench of events.
The silk indifferent sky.

One sunlit day, you drove our truck,
wheelchair in back, on a lazy interstate,
when a smug triumvirate of Harleys
vroomed: behind us, beside us, past us,
over the hill be damned!

In that churned-up throbbing wake,
you grabbed my hand.

OLD BLACK WATER

We stopped at a small deserted beach
by the great Mississippi, just as the Doobies'
cassette clicked on. You opened your door
and nearly sank in the deep soft sand.

With your crutch and cane,
and some leaning on me, we staggered
to the trees.

At the edge, we breathed the dark,
        crude, riparian scent
of spicy, juicy, alien green,
        and searched the bowling-ball sky
to wish on the very first star.

We hauled that rich, evocative night,
the thrill of our trip, back across the
continent, dark clouds scuffing the sky.

Rainbows painted a song lost to sight
as soon as we turned around.

Still we kept on rolling, in no hurry at all…

THE STUDY OF BIRDS

We start out as little bits of disconnected
dust. No, we start out as birds.
~ Naomi Shihab Nye

You felt a kinship with birds. Wrens'
     rapid wingstrokes from our bluebird house,
harmonizing joy and scolding, trilling melodies
     on the spot. Bending their legs
to rhythms fluttering in their heads.

The large snowy owl in the park at Kahlotus.
     A merlin landing on a rail beside you,
as you look up from a book. Flickers, red-shafted
     like the dawn. Collared doves,
on sky-colored powerlines, sit on air.

Cedar bushes bustling with waxwings.
Hawks circling Dubois. Sandhill cranes…

You enjoyed the study of birds, but described a class
     outing, the professor's gaze in the branches,
you lagging behind, harboring a snake
     you'd caught, in a binoculars case.
Well, reptiles were the first birds…

Once we woke to a bird you'd never heard
     before. The newness, freshness, youth
of it all! Joy rose like hot-air balloons!
     Dawn fluffed its chances,
promising something new.

~ for my cousin Donna

18

SCULPTING CASTLES IN THE AIR

All those years of laundromats.
        Moms yelling, smacking
their kids. Tears, including mine.
        I tried to read but stared
at shirts in dryers arm-wrestling,
        strangling each other,
flailing blind. That day in Safeway
        when a child was slapped
a few aisles back, a blur, *I cried*
        silently, with little him or her.

The specialist didn't know if it was the polio,
        or the x-rays to kill the polio,
but a final test told us to adopt.
        Paperwork, physicals. Three long years
of miracle, scraped across the sky.
        Had we been dropped?

The Orkney Islands! you say, out of the blue.
        We could scrimp and go,
set this pining behind. Viking sagas,
        standing stones, castles in salt air.
Recitals in cathedrals. Shakespeare staged
        near hallowed bridges
arching ancient streams.

But on a dusty hoof-pocked backroad,
        fresh essence of the U.S.A.,
we passed a saltlick castle, sculpted
        by cow tongues. *A castle, in salt*
and air, floating our shaky dreams…

IN NO TIME

Three days old, dark hair, fingernails busy traveling
his face. Smiles blooming on ours. After twelve
years of marriage, we adopted a baby,

bought a house, a dryer, and TV. First night he slept
on a pillow in a cardboard box. Sweet innocence
dreamed in soft ballooning sighs.

Brush me into shooting stars, comb me blissful,
buoyant, scatterbrained! Your face let the sun waltz in!

You'd stand against a wall to hold him. Of course
you loved him ~ you smoked your pipe outside!

> You: *Come on, we don't have all day.*
> Three-year-old: *Yes us do!*

He'd clamber onto your lap, your lame leg chafing
'til he stilled. His head on your shoulder as you
read, read, read to him. *Again* was his favorite word.

Our dog digging under a fence. A chorus frog
rescued from a muddy cow-hoof print. A cat
who clowned in our garage.

Two parakeets disparaging our choice
of shows.

Our curve of earth swayed anew. Your spine
began to waver ~ *polio, round two.*

II. *UNCERTAINTIES*

We are the river,
made of rain, waves fumbling

end over end...

WHAT FATE MADE US MOVE
TO STATES BURNING ASH?

"Trees fell with a crackling thud"
~ Marjane Ambler

Where could we find a leopard sky, or a few
quail-feathered clouds? Some cure-all luminescence

in this frightful choking pall?
Yellowstone ~ close, as a crow flies ~ swelled

to a lightning-furnace belching flames, smoke for miles,
shattering its summer trees.

Our toddler, out for only minutes, cried for his shadow.
The ache of a dog bark stoked and churned

    the hollow plunge of night.

You bore asthmatic flare-ups, lungs
waxing and waning, nipping the grasp of our days.

What fate made us move to states bursting ash,
for weeks or months of blight?

We planted ourselves inside. You sketched a kingfisher,
wrote book reviews. I took notes, from fear:

    The wind's disrupting everything.
      Here comes a gust of deer!

SUN COMES UP THROUGH A TUMBLEWEED

Last night, your breathing

overshot haunted, you
turned left, right, nowhere

to run. I held you tight

'til dawn spread
        another blanket

and cold fear raged

      ragged

into light.

THE BLUE HAP/HAZARD SKY

Tonight the stars
      flake and groan

igniting our dark
      snakelike road.

I follow the red-lit ambulance
      hurdling to emergency.

If only I could breathe for you!!

The hall bustling with gurneys,
disinfectant, your haunting gasps.

You lie looking up, at pulsing blades
      of light.

I focus on ancient calm.

Cold and immense,
      a radiance, a cure!

I cry. Freefall, recovery!
      The blue hap/hazard sky.

A LANGUAGE OF SHADOWS

Bright green lawn, shadows out the window. A young buck,
    antlers velvet golden, strides toward the dawn.

    Years you'd push out of chairs, ripping tendons
    in your good arm. Letters of medical necessity,

    shoulder surgery. So little the doctors could stitch
    together. Four weeks' occupational therapy
    in Thermop.

    Staff called you a model patient. But all your life
    you knew this day would come.
    Rolling, sliding, instead of walking.

Stricken with polio. *Confined* to a wheelchair.

    How like a venomous viper, or an infamous boa,
    our language can *strike* or *constrict!*

        No words could find your tongue!

    You'll need an electric scooter, basket in front,
    PVC pipe for your cane and crutch, a ramp,
    a sliding-board to transfer, some faith

    in yourself, trust in the world, a fold-up lift
    for the back of the car...

Beneath the white-tailed morning moon, a doe and her young
    nibble silence in the draw....

ANGLES OF UNCERTAINTY

The gods, you told me, knew you'd fall a lot,
so they made your kneecaps hard as rock.

Your world's always shifting. It must feel like treading
on shattered ice plates rimming a massive lake.

I was waiting in line with groceries, lunch.
You were home, pushing stacks of journals
with your forearm crutch.

You wavered scary, lost your balance, hit
the carpet hard. Your face in scabs and red-dark burns.

Pain chomped your left hand, your little finger
sprained. Our son helped you to the scooter,
got you ice and meds, looked for the finger splint…

You suffer a painful icy-burn. Your ulnar nerve
is moved to the inside of your arm.

Goldfinches erupt overhead, their bills
clicking castanets.

A large pot sits in the foreground, lid bumping rhythms,
a kettledrum spewing messages from the stew inside.

Cold edges, bold trajectories, angles of uncertainty,
jolt our future to its knees, appealing to the steam.

THROUGH KING COBRA EYES

My mind, a stream meandering,
        let some blurry daydream
tug me along. Then I spotted you ahead,
        zigzagging through the human race,
heading for the door.

Maybe you grew tired of this deafening
        crowd. (I know I did!) Maybe
you wanted to see Komodo Dragons,
        crocodiles out back?

Whoa! Wait! Our son and I
        saw the King Cobra, bored
and lounging in its space, rise slowly,
        swelling its neck to hooded
against the glass.

This twelve-foot venomous Malaysian king
        tasted the oppressive air, keeping its
eyes on you. The rest of us were shuffling,
        common. But in your scooter,
you rode serpentine!

This supple reptile felt your freedom.
        We ran to fetch you.
Seems you were a natural.
        You made each other's day!

NORMALCY

You roll through life, in a store,
on a trip, as normal as anyone,
harboring wishes and wounds, rushing,
then stranded, making your way
to the front of the line

just when the window slams down.

Every so often, we're awed by the random
acts of strangers, who pay for your brisket,
jump into a pool to help you, lift you,
pains-takingly, over a large stone block

so you'd see the canyon below.

High school student trucks at Wendy's,
boys impatient, inventive, honking
and beeping a freeform cadence, pleased
with themselves, their innovative tunes

encompassing us, our distant presence

as we eat tacos, in a hurry to get
back to work, the rhythm of rolling,
of being alive, in what must have been

a normal spring.

FLASHBACKS

The ground lay black, lethargic, for years.
Tightfisted clouds plagued the stoic pond.

I couldn't get home in time!
  I know you were terrified!

Early April, positively brisk. I was in a meeting
most of the afternoon, phone in my desk.

You left three messages!!!
  I listened heedfully, absorbing your urgency.

A man lit a fire in the reeds by the water, to show
his little daughter the goldfish he'd put in. A flare
crocheted its way through the brush.

You sat in your recliner,
  watching it approach our trees!

You couldn't turn your legs toward the scooter. All
you could do was call and wait! Someone helped you
into a truck. *Neighbors and firemen battled the flames.*

After school, our son fought newer flares. I raced home
and stomped on sparks *quivering across the drive…*

Some days, awaiting the scritch and pop of fickle rain,
the red vetch rattles its noisy pods in the sweeping
brazen wind

and that very fire
  leaps and bellows through my brain.

UNDER GOD & THE SLIP OF MOON

The moon, just four days old,
          was gently rocking crescent
as Van the Man stole offstage
          with his last harmonica wail.
The wheelchair section, up
          in the nippy concession zone,
had left a mid-June chill
          brewing in our bones. You worked
the truck, nip and tuck,
          into the long, slow, winding descent.
The bumper-to-bumper surge
          of stop-start, stop-on-a-dime traffic
tested how fast you could clutch
          your jeans, to raise your foot, pedal
to pedal, gas to brake, over and over
          again in the dark. One miss,
and the slam, mash, or snap of a bumper
          would rattle the cars before and after,
the scene forever roiling, bashing the script
          in our minds, our bodies internally
combusting with screams. In the still of the cab,
          you spun the gears of resolve,
under God and the slip of moon,
          the rhythm of stop-start, stop-on-a-dime
bearing us safely to the bottom,
          muscles tiring, the journey thrilling
not for its ending but for its beginning.
          Memories unwinding, satisfying.
The *Moondance* braiding flute and bass.
          The breath it takes to make music.
The music that takes
          our breath away...

TITANIUM RIVER

Although there was no river,
      except for a trickle of people
coming and going,
      I sat long enough
in that waiting-room
      to picture the Seine
through Monet's eyes,
      the light rippling,
splintering reflections, then draining
      as your face appeared,
brush-stroked, patchy,
      bleary from surgery.

      You'd fallen at home, fractured
      an ankle, seen three hospitals
      that week. A metallic rod, pins,
      plates and three-way screws
      now occupy that leg. Time
      to recover, three weeks in Casper.
      Several more at home.

We flow below dark-bellied clouds
      dissolving on the road,
long wiggles of dusk preying on us,
      part of the straggling crowd.
Trucks take turns do-si-doing.
      Pronghorn gossip
along the waning edge.
      The day's on its side, draining
the sky. We are the river, made of rain,
      waves fumbling, end over end,
doing our darndest to shine.

REFLECTIONS

A big clunky boot, with its hook-and-loopy
velvet-grippy tabs, holds your healing leg.
One of your wheelchair motors dies.
Repaired so many times. Parts are hard to find.

You're using your old, half-broken scooter.
The struggle's not over, yet your bones do mend.
A new wheelchair and lift arrive in Cheyenne.
Everything takes longer. So much to learn.

> *Morning shimmers on our sliding glass door.*
> *An oriole keeps pecking its reflection,*
> *flapping up, down, up and pecking again.*

On a steep ramp at work, you and your briefcase
slide off the chair. Your other ankle's broken!
Can't put your weight on it for two long months.
Left, now right boot, day boot, night!

The boots, rough, scratchy, sweaty. Your sense
of imbalance swells. Each new dawn gnaws
what confidence remains. Your ankle heals,
but your foot's turned slightly to the side.

Your hip and knee feel the strain.
You can no longer stand.

> *I lean over the back of your chair, wrap my arms*
> *around you, our hearts fluttering, heads*
> *nesting together, reflecting, for awhile…*

LIKE A COMET TO STARE AT SIDEWAYS

Children are the best people.
~ Helen Potts

Adults felt uncomfortable, needed to joke. Always
the same joke: *Gee, I wish I had one of those!*

Or they'd glance and smile away, awkwardly,
scurrying into the hushed-up day.

Sometimes, they'd gaze above your head
at the seemingly hypnotic sky.

Remember the waitress who stared at *me*, icily,
asking what *you'd* like to eat?! We felt that slight
like a sharpened knife.

Children looked straight at you. You loved 'em!
What's wrong with you? they'd ask, or *Why
are you sitting down?*

They were nine-out-of-ten parts wonder, energy.
Their quick press against your arm said mountains.

Bless the parents who didn't whisk them away
in a cloud of dust, because they'd *bother* you!

You shift your chair to rabbit speed. A roadside
sunflower, nodding sideways in the wind,
waves us on and on...

YANK UP THE MOON: A TURNIP RANT

Re: the American Disabilities Act, Title III:
Public Accommodations & Commercial Facilities

Never know what we'll find in hotels down the line...

In case of fire, use the stairs. Abandon the disabled
in a blast of flaming air?!

Power failure. It's bad behavior
to book the paralyzed

on any floor but first, unless there bursts
a savior never advertised!

The room met our specs on the call, but now much later,
the chair's in the hall. Won't fit in the elevator!

Roll-in shower, they state with pride, but spoil it
when the toilet has no space to park beside.

Doors swing out in front of doors, even in suite deals.
Bulky coffee tables block the way for wheels.

We plan to yank the moon up, relax and celebrate,
but deem the room a turnip with which to acclimate.

No one test-drives any bedsides, or wheels chairs
to a balcony. Shrugged-off guidelines are the fine lines

of a blinkered apathy!

IN GOOD WEATHER

People still remember us
loading your wheelchair into the pickup
after your adjunct classes. They'd stop in awe,
as though we were a circus act
performing for the parking lot.
Our routine did have a certain flair, if only
we had bowed or curtsied, at strategic spots.

*But this was real life, so we did no*t!

You raised your chair seat, grabbed the bar
on the dash, and rode your board's sliding disk
up to the truck's front seat. *You were the conjurer
in the cab!* I'd set the footrest down, lower the chair,
align it with the truck bed, turn it off, and raise its arms.
You pressed the remote UP, OUT, and DOWN,
delivering the lift to me. I'd attach the straps
and aim the chair. You pressed UP and IN.

Wheelchair flying across the sky!

I'd swivel the chair to face front. You'd press DOWN.
I'd guide it beyond the toolbox, between the wheel wells,
unlatch the tailgate, climb in, lower the arms, jump down,
shut the tailgate, and toss the footrest in. Then home
to repeat the steps, all the other way 'round…

And that, in good weather, was that. Ta-da!

ON NOT LOOKING AT DEVILS TOWER

Straight in front of our eyes
you spy a branch of young
ponderosa, in a doghair thicket

with a nest of five
ruby-crowned kinglet chicks
fed by their father,
proud royalty with a bold red cap.

Listen to their hungry cheeps!

You tilt your wheelchair back, blessed
by happenstance.

Trekkers on the trail

just two feet away

chitchat and gaze

off the ledge.

WIND RACING THROUGH YOUR HAIR

I'd have made that damn thing fly if I could.
~ Mike Skiba

In August, in April, on Christmas Eve ~ anytime ~
a wheelchair can grow achy or feisty, or, like C-3PO,
just shut itself down.

Time and again a gearbox, heavy batteries, left
or right motors, died without regard for you.
Static plied its tricks.

Mike lay on the floor, rewiring an old joystick,
a many-colored journey in the galaxy under the seat.

One snowy night the power quit, trapping you in
your electric recliner. Mike arrived, dragged a bench,
helped you tilt into your chair,

then invented a rolling inverter: big battery, DC to
AC, with cord, plug, and dolly for the next dark time.

But what if your chair could convert to a spaceship?
Or, better, a Gee Bee, your favorite plane!
Open cockpit, joystick control.

Wind racing through your hair...

THE GHOST OF NOT DRIVING

The ways of the future are less complex
than the lightning flow of rivers in Africa,
or the delicate map of a butterfly wing.

You were good at driving. Careful
anticipation of traffic, brake lights, deer
or careless people stepping off a curb.

But you struggled for years to start on a hilltop
without first sliding back. You could see
the downward spiral, motorcycle

to van. You dared not lose your grip
on the wheel or the world. Red-yellow-green
lights of rosebush leaves, just hanging on.

The ghost appeared late in life. It witnessed
your struggle on a trip back from Casper
when we were too close to a long tractor-trailer

and you couldn't pull the handbrake to slow
and let the traffic pass. I reached across the console,
both hands coming from an angle...

and together we didn't crash!
A van shouted *disability*, a frailty
you'd been trying to hide.

One day you practiced getting in and out
as a passenger, so I could drive should the need arise.
And, contrary to years of discussion, you *did not say*

that would kill you.

ANYTHING IS A LUXURY

You rode the ramp into our van, weary
from constantly battling the wind,
coaxing me to shop in the mall,
find something I'd like. Anything at all.

Bright lights, noise. Endless hangers of pants
and tops, swaying like strangers in a line,
trying not to touch. A dress the rhythm
of flouncy skirts whispered columbine
summer nights. I turned the tag. Back
on the rack, little luxury!

I climbed into the van exhausted, set your
wheel-locks front and back, snapped
your seatbelt, and drove. You'd been watching
the parking lot exit, a man bent
in the pummeling heat.

> *Anything Will Help*
> read the handmade sign. No one
> had stopped to hand him *Anything.*

A surge of cars at a well-mannered pace
erased him with their dust.

You asked me to stop, then held out a five-
dollar bill. The well of tears when he took it
told how much that little meant.

SKY GONE MOODY

Plays or concerts: in the handicap-only section: No
seats for a partner or friend…

Old classic bookstores: No ramps or public elevators,
only stairs. You who loved to browse the shelves!

Telephone pole, smack in the middle of a sidewalk!
You turn around, ride your chair into traffic

which treats you like a pinball, and find smashed
or mis-matched curb-cuts…

A small car sits on the crosshatch space, after our
celebratory lunch. How to let the ramp down, to load

your chair! Deep sigh. Jot down the license number,
go back inside…

Riverboat cruise, planned highlight of a trip billed accessible –
was Not!

Handicap signs in a small parking zone, up to their
chins in snow plowed onto their spaces…

The sky gone moody, rearranges its clouds…

I GOT MY HEAD IN FRONT OF THE TIGER

I'd been watching howler monkeys
swing through slats of sun's zebraic light.

I stopped to gaze at a male tomato frog
asleep. The warm air made *me* sleepy, too.

At the tigers, I saw a man in back
trying for a camera shot. I sped

across the crowd, arriving right by you ~
and crouched.

I'd jostled you! I couldn't see that you,
wheelchair deep in tree shade, were aiming, too!

> To frame a tiger, its blossom of a face
> peering from captivity, antiquity, at you.

No way could I foresee your phone (your hands
would shake!) or the depth of your angry mood!

The tiger turned and shouldered up the slope.

> The luxurious fire of its slumber,
> shadow-striped in flagrant camouflage.

I was sorry, over and over.

Your silence roared!

FLIGHT

You pause on the edge of our bed,
a sun-striped deity, pain waking
and crawling your spine,
then pivot
onto your sliding-board,
and stop
midway to your wheelchair,
staring at the sky.
You don't look at me.

You okay, honey?

There's a red airplane.
Might be a Piper Cub.
A light monoplane, one pair
of wings. Seats two in tandem,
like a bicycle built that way.
Can make a perfect
three-point
landing…

You okay, honey?!

You don't look at me…

III. FOLDING

A scan
will forecast suffering

or chance of giddy shine..

A BRAND-NEW DARK

The drop in light's intensity, your energy, that fall.
An increase in doctors, devices. Home health.
PT. OT. CT. MRI. Pressure wound. Mess and laundry.
Scares and ambulance calls.

All anyone says is *Up the meds.* (*Let you sleep your life away.*)
Your bright eyes lose focus. Fingers crunch up. Tremors
rule your hands. You argue half-jokingly with Cortana,
a voice recognition app: "I said parity, NOT parrot tree!"

    No more jolly rivalry: Scrabble, Big Boggle, Jeopardy.

Even with hearing aids, you can't hear the raspy
chatter-trill of redwing blackbirds on the pond, ready
for trips to Mexico.

    Pain and silence shrink your world.

We lie in bed, wheelchair charging, wound vac droning by
our pillows. All that coiled-up tubing re-taped to your thigh.
All the churning hope that soon this hellish wound will dry!

The redwings rise to ancestral trails, weaving and calling,
finding their way, as we do, through a brand-new dark.

THE SNOW'S FRAYED EDGES FINGER NO SUN

You're a frail, burdened slope
beneath our flowered quilt. A coarse
    rush of breath
shot with misery
and barbarous wheezy gasps.

Tiny hand-sewn stitches, white
on white, baby steps,
    sinuous tracery,
on fading lilac blocks. I feign calm
so you'll stay calm.

The snow, blue unreality,
fingers no sun. I seek
    tomorrow's answers
in low criss-crashing
patchwork clouds

tight-knit winter branches,
our cold stony road.
    A scan
will forecast suffering
or chance of giddy shine.

Meanwhile you snuggle
toward me. I stroke
    your brow.
A threadbare silence snags our story,
and lets the shadows grow.

- for Kristina

EROSIONAL RADIANCE

Caregiving is a daily exercise
in making miracles happen.
~Susan J. Tweit

Your voice frail, barely audible, yet your sense
of humor fills a room.
Angoraphobia = Fear of sweaters!

Your hand's so shaky on the joystick,
your chair's scraped the wainscoting
all down the hall. *I don't mind.*

I rise drowsily, sort your many pills, help
you get dressed and into your chair again.
You are a mountain in erosional radiance.

You talk me through trimming your moustache
and beard. A bad fall crumbles your spine.

You can no longer sit up.

We eat our dinner in bed. You brush your teeth
lying down. *You don't laugh anymore.*

The sky's a bulky woolen, cable-stitched
wobbly twist of light. A soft *who-o-o* from a great
horned owl. December flies away too soon.

The tenderness of our last kiss
    before the hospital,
        warms the winter moon.

NERO WOLFE & THE CURTAIN
THAT MUST BE OBEYED

No way you can see the moon fading
on the snow. Your bed faces The Curtain.

You doze off in mid-sentence, waking
with an acute non-sequitur, unsure
why everyone in the room starts laughing.

An ambulance brought you to this town, this
hospital, for debriding your pressure wound.
You're exhausted, uneasy, slipping away.

Tubes in nostrils, a PICC line, a bag
hanging down. You have a MRSA infection,
IV antibiotics, meds for pain. Different doctors
different days. Your nights grow long.

Behind The Curtain, staff and visitors don gowns,
masks and gloves. Handwashing, no hugs.

You, who'd come home from a library
exhaling books throughout the rooms, can't read
a mystery on your ebook, even in huge font.

I shrink Nero Wolfe and make the characters
speak in distinct voices, out loud ~ apparently
out *too* loud! The Curtain shouts *Hush!*

When I turn back, you're asleep.

FEBRUARY, WYOMING: THE IMMENSITY

Remember the sky you were born under,
know each of the stars' stories.
    ~ Joy Harjo

I leave the rehab/nursing-home,
where an ambulance transported you.
I'm saddened by your helplessness
and mine.

I stop at the roadside mailboxes.
Kill the engine but not the headlights.
Walk to box eight, metallic chill. Unlock,
gather ads and bills, then turn and stare

       at the immensity of Dark.

No moon tonight, no milky way.
A huge splatter of brilliant stars!
Imagine. No, listen! Old radio chatter.
Space music splutter. The wishes
I wasted over the years...

I want to describe it for you, but you can't
reach your phone (or find the call-button
pinned to your blanket!).

With a fistful of mail, I walk to my car,
memorizing the sky, to share with you
tomorrow, like a flower, or the icicle dripping
from the feeder outside your window

       in the immensity of Light.

BLUE BEGINS WITH AN ORANGE SHRIEK

March. 2:52 a.m. My phone rings. I'm right beside you
in a dream, your face on fire, your back screaming
to leave the rest-home, hallways choked with patients
inching along in treadle machines…

A nurse on her rounds finds you breathing with effort,
running a slight temperature. She'd already called
an ambulance. Bright sawblades romp beneath my lids.
Migraine aura! *None of this is a dream!*

I sit in the forever-waiting room, dressed in what I could
grab, the TV and candy machines failing
as companions. Then pacing, crying, I watch the sky
hook moonlight to morning, then turn inside-out.

Drab to blue, an orange streak. Sirens! All of this unreal.
Gershwin's first few notes of *Rhapsody* collide with O'Keefe's
Orange and Red Streak. Blue begins with an orange shriek,
and *Orange* gapes blue-green.

The sirens start in my head, slide to my heart, and *stop me*
in my tracks. If not for a nurse's vigilance, your future'd
have been in rest-home covid-lockdown. You'd never
see home, again…

~ for Nurse Tracy, Thank you!

HOME, YOU SAY, REPEATEDLY

Your bed's in a back room, a different
hospital. You're scared, disoriented, weak.
The view from your window, a concrete wall.

Your pressure wound's on a new vac. Doctors
need to see the two-week treatment through.

In the ICU, they monitor your heart, the vac,
your breathing, and try to sit you up.
 One day they rush you back to your room.
Some people need the ICU more than you do.
The first covid patients have arrived.

I spend some nights on a cot, and run to the desk
for help when no one hears you call.

All those childhood fears, when doctors spoke
of polio, all the things you'd never do. You slump
into despair.

Infection, inflammation, more oxygen.
Gloves and gowns still come and go.

Home, you say, repeatedly. They don't listen.

Home (to die), you whisper ~ and they hear.

~ for Echo, who oversaw this release

LANDSCAPE WITH SNOW & BIRDFEEDERS

No memory, it seems, without loss
& high winds.
                                        ~ James McKean

March in Wyoming, eleven degrees, ten. The cottonwoods
mere wraiths against a soft blue marbled bend of sky.

Happiness wheeled your hospital bed up the shoveled ramp.
You saw our home, our family, through grateful-weary tears!

Our son bought you feeders to view from your window.
They just fed the wind. Such hope in a land of greenlessness
where birds that spend the winter only sing in spring.

Once you woke me for water, then reached for my hand
through the rungs, holding tight 'til you slipped off to sleep
again. A beautiful energy rose and splashed the night.

                        ****

You fight dying, sleep in daylight, wake each night for pills,
wanting water you forget you can't swallow, backrubs, a tilt
of mattress, blankets or quilts pulled up or back down.

More light! Dragged by the wind, slammed into trees,
darkness feeds your vivid-scary dreams.

One night you're so afraid: *Someone's at the door!* I check
them all, finding only branches clobbering the moon.
We'd better tell Brenda, you say, nodding back to sleep.

~ for Nurse Brenda, with Hospice Care

SWEET COMIC RELIEF

Our three-year-old grandson
spied his father

squatting by a closet
sorting drills and wrenches

on the floor. He asked
what his dad was doing.

Looking for a tool,
came the answer.

Toos! His little face
set the house aglow.

We need toos to fix Papa!

- *for Wylder*

FOLDING

the comfy things
that go on shelves

sheets, sweaters,
towels, I feel

a slight control.
You hurt and I

can't save you, can't write
this stiff disharmony

jarring my small world.
It galls and scares me

that you don't get well.
The sky's a snagged

gray shrug. I wander room
to room

thinking nothing, as dusk
whisks everything

away.

~ for Muriel & Craig

53

HOW LIKE A WHISPER

The neighbors' smoke-white mare
snorted, her first morning there,
like a pull-string push mower
trying to start. She spooked
as our blinds
whinnied up the glass. Stared
and turned dark eyes away.

> *She radiated patience*
> *while you struggled to breathe,*
> *contorted with pain.*

***

> *Without you now, her slow walk*
> *across the pasture*
> *feels like balm to me…*

She's a moving constant I rely on.
Stands firm in snowfall.
Beneath big storm clouds
she lights up, a bright moon
nibbling sparkly weeds.
Like you, she slips into a fog.

Except you leave no trace!

> *How like a whisper*
> *your life just*
> *trails away…*

IV. *THE SHOCK OF GRIEF*

I am not alive nor dead.
I'm half of Us, something caught

between...

WHY AM I STILL BREATHING?

I can't watch this, I said

       and walked to the dining room.

I forgot I had opened the blinds!

       They wheeled that zippered bag

down the ramp.

       You out of your body.

Me out of my mind!

INSIDE GRIEF

There is no paneled door
to midnight.
Everyone sweeps a path
to an unlit window,
under an icy sky. No need
to knock. We find ourselves
inside.

I AM NOT THAT LIZARD

Once in Tucson you lifted a lizard
from our stove, set it outside
on the dirt, and stepped back smiling.
The lizard turned, ran straight
to your shoes, and looked up.

Flying?! it seemed to say. *Do that again!*

Well, I am not that lizard
now that you are gone.
I'm the lizard we saw
in the wide shadeless desert.
The lizard a loggerhead shrike
had pierced to the quick
on a fencepost alongside a trail.

EVERY WINDOW OF MY MARROW

We were *Us* forever, back in time. *Us*
for time to come.

You are Nowhere now,
but you are Everywhere!

I am not alive, nor dead. I'm half of *Us*,
something caught between. Something

without legs or brain. A thunderous
beating heart in a hollow quivering wall.

I'm sorry for everything I never said
or thanked you for. The times I didn't

understand. I'm sitting on a panther's
back, willing its spots to shine.

I'm a vine, making it up as I go along
in many-petaled grief. Oh, to have your hand

in reach! I can't live in this house without you,
though you breathe from every corner,

every window of my marrow. Every shadow
on the lawn. All I have are raindrops typing.

These nights of empty cow-skull moons.
Sequence shatters. Words trip over one

another, iguanas in a desert zoo. I should
leave. I can't! I don't want to! I need to!

I am Nowhere, now...

UTTER LONELINESS

The sky's a pallid blue.   The earth
screams green   wasting
lavish scent.   The day's back
is turned to me.   I'm not meant
to hear   grass
or leaves grow,   not meant
to conjure up   the sun
or utter loneliness, except
in   faltering   tongue.

I WRITE THE MOON'S MAD FUMBLE

We are migrating to another platform.
Changing all the legal agreements that apply
to you. Synching your data to a cloud.
                              ~ no-reply emails

I'm thousands of years old, trying to speak for all
humanity. I cry at kindness and deep loss, the heartless

ways our world can scam us. The cold rain, wind,
the heat that's stripping glaciers to their bones.

People are homeless. Homebound. Burned out.
War-bound. Making a home alone. I have

Long Covid, Complicated Grief, Internet Distress:
LCCGID. Too much weight for that single vowel, I.

I write the moon's mad fumble to romp in rivers,
shine fangs of light on waterfalls, hear their stories,
grab the cannoli, and run like the wind…

In all this rain and ruin, spring's first meadowlark!

FORGING THROUGH THE FOG

Only a crash of thunder, or a pheasant's croaky
call, can still the noisy collared doves.

How light the shadows, how heavy the light.

I spot a young bull snake, a rope of fluid
sunshine, afternooning in the fog.

My mind all stones with river patterns, feathers
moving, one synapse at a time.

The rocks we stood on. The rocks we threw
when we couldn't understand.

The moments we want back!

You're at peace now, though I'll need
some time to catch up.

Grief, a feather's push from healing. Healing,
a feather's push from grief...

A pair of cranes floats by, science-fiction large,
and I a grain of sand. I'm proud to be this grain

who saw them soar and settle, and heard their
raucous calm release them from the fog.

Lighter than air, I brush the sorrow from my hair.

WE, I KEEP THINKING

A patter of snow
on yesterday's glut. The sun
blinks halfheartedly,
blinding just the same.

I balk like the daffodils
I dug in, years ago.
Thirsty, wary...

The sun trickles over, and snow
powders through again. A mist
rides the puddled road. Mud
from my tires leaps like frogs.

We'd seen fewer daffodils
every year.
Thinner, wanting...

Your death of toxic wound,
crumbling spine, asthma,
crashed the covid scare. Strangled
choices from computer voices
cuff me to a chair.

We, I keep thinking.
Our, I keep saying.
Now it's down...

to me.

~ for Ann

63

LISTENING TO "THE PILGRIM"

Dollar Brand/Abdullah Ibrahim

Piano notes, full-handed, slow,
soothe the reservoir sky blue

      then a riffle ~ a lightning strike!
      Dissonance shrills the air. Yet hear:

A dulcet-throated flute-bird
broadcasts his love, his longing,

spilling poignant secrets,
passionate belief, onto watery quiver,

      the reddest sundown prayer...

PURE EVENING

Take a bite of it,
this cake of rich lawn.

Lick the goop of frosting
horizon.

Smell the faint white
cusp of candle on top.

Someone is born each day,
each night

someone dies.
It all seems simple

this evening, this
even-ing out of poise,

this purity we dare to breathe

      and then
                    go
                          on…

V. *A SPLASH OF SUN*

Tenderness
speaks to us

of fleeting certainty...

A STILLNESS ROSE

First hike down   a stumble,
new boots in bluish light.
I stand up dizzy, staring

past rippled stone to water,
through rippling water to stone,
the setting sun

angling prismatic.

Full-moon switchbacks,
purple shadow walls,
the light changes

and I start over differently.
I need the turns, the time,
the river's blinding roar

imprinted on my mind.

RECALLING US AS SPARKLE

I can see a speck in the sky
that reaches out for me, and so I know
it is Earth, and I am not on it.
                    ~ Sonya Plenefisch

Time flows and flowers through black holes. I listen
to fire calling distant stars. The galaxies bounce with
memories, tugging each other's spiral arms.

> *First anniversary, canyon-rim cabin, mist settling*
> *heavenly, heavily. Oops, there goes Temple Butte!*

I look for my place in the universe. Our planet
bows to star-buckled promises, what's new,
what's ancient as the sigh of dusk.

> *I wander like birds circling in thermals, like fish*
> *drawn to lights in a pond, then I fall back into space.*

I'd forgotten the garden-window geode-sparkle
of our planet's only moon. The spicy desert rain.
The lighthouse, from here, a tiny candle jittering a flame.

> *Recalling Us as sparkle. Your physical presence*
> *on earth.   I must remember to breathe...*

INTO THE MYSTIC

Your voice lit up my room, a moon
disentangling from the night.

I wasn't sleeping. And I'm not making
this up!

A year ago you'd breathed your last!

I'd been reading, laid the book on my
bedside table, slid under the covers, then

I heard my name in deep reverberance,
and saw two syllables

CAR-OL, each in capitals, all emphasis,
no stress. No heater noise, no human voice,
no dream, no yell.

My name came loud from down the hall,
on the roof, or from a giant star...

I can't pull the magical from the mundane
or logical, or musical notes from their
various intervals.

I clasp this night with the soft abandon
of a silken waterfall, and the thunderous
miracle

     of your late night call.

REBLOSSOMING

Crack, Rumble. Boom!
Fireworks, red blossoming

reblossoming, so high in the evening
from the end of our driveway

so dazzlingly LOUD.

Crack, Rumble. Boom!
Our fires bloom such energy,
clear memories…

The day we met. Now your life's
celebration, dedication. I know

you can hear our JOY!

~ for Brandon

MOVING STORIES

Andy lives in your heart, not in your house.
~ Marilû Chapela Duncan

Everything tells a story as it walks out the door
to the overlong moving van. I listen and yank
the movers' sleeves. Can they hear this?!

Rhinoceri bolt from their spaces. Native arts
and crafts, framed paintings jump from walls.
Cowboy hats tip their beaded bands. Antique
clocks and watches chime while time takes flight.
Old pens, bottles of colorful inks slosh goodbye…

We thought we could hold onto things…

I open doors to memories, weep silently
in the stripped-free room without a bed, then
check the garage. That first time I drove back
from Casper, knowing you wouldn't be
waiting at home, the sun staring me down.

The depth of sadness on a late afternoon…

Leaving our home of thirty-plus years, now
three-plus more, alone. Boxing up and wondering:
Who was I then?   Who am I now?!
What will I need where I've never been?

*I know you would want me
                to be happy
                        on this passage…*

ACKNOWLEDGMENTS

Thanks to the editors of these journals where the following poems first appeared, some in a slightly different version.

JOURNALS:

Duck Head Journal: "We, I Keep Thinking."
Front Range Review: "A Loveliness" and "Spray."
Gyroscope Review: "The Blue Hap/Hazard Sky" (as
    "Weightlessness").
Mason Street Review: "The Snow's Frayed Edges Finger No Sun."
Muddy River Poetry Review: "Glory Days" and "La Jolla
    Weekend."
The Muse (McMaster University): "Nero Wolfe & the Curtain That
    Must Be Obeyed" and "Titanium River."
The Ocotillo Review: "On Not Looking at Devils Tower."
Panoplyzine: "Old Black Water."
Parks & Points & Poetry: "A Stillness Rose."
Provo Canyon Review. "Listening to 'The Pilgrim'."
Shorts Magazine: "February, Wyoming: The Immensity" (as
    "February, Wyoming: Seven PM").
Talking River Review: "Anything Is a Luxury," "I Got My Head in
    Front of the Tiger," "Like a Comet to Stare at Sideways," and
    "Step into a Geode."
Weber: The Contemporary West: "Helping Snakes across the Road"
    and "How Like a Whisper."
WyoPoets News: "Inside Grief" (as "Grief").

ANTHOLOGIES:

Wayfinding: Parks & Points & Poetry, ed. by Amy & Derrick Wright.
    Finishing Line Press, 2021. "A Stillness Rose."

PERMISSIONS

Thanks to these authors for permission to quote from their work:

Page 4: Danusha Laméris, from her poem "Riding Bareback," in *The Moons of August* (Autumn House Press, 2014) p. 58.

Page 13: Gerard Manley Hopkins (1844-1889), from his poem "Spring" (public domain).

Page 18: Naomi Shihab Nye, from the introduction to her book *19 Varieties of Gazelle: Poems of the Middle East* (Greenwillow Books, 2002) p. xii.

Page 32: Marjane Ambler, from her book *Yellowstone Has Teeth* (Riverbend Publishing, 2013), p. 164.

Page 46: Susan J. Tweit, from her book *Bless the Birds: Living with Love in a Time of Dying* (She Writes Press, 2021), p.80.

Page 48: Joy Harjo, from her poem "Remember," in *She Had Some Horses* (Thunder's Mouth Press, 1983), p.40.

Page 51: James McKean, from his poem "Middlestand Ferry," in *We Are the Bus* (Texas Review Press, 2012), p.48.

Page 68: Sonya Hartley Plenefisch, from her poem "The First Kingdom: I. Coronation," in *Memoirs of a King* (Sonya Plenefisch, 2016), unpaged.

THANKS

Thanks to the friends who at some point in time agreed (whether they remember or not) to let me use a phrase from our conversations: Helen Potts, Mike Skiba, and Marilú Chapela Duncan.

And to Muriel White, Darlene Farrow, and Brenda Benavente, who each found and returned old letters or postcards Andy and I had sent over the years. A wild paperstorm of memories!

And to the supportive readers, some of whom have their kind thoughts included in this book: Betsy, Echo, Gus, John, Kathleen, Laurie, Lynne, Tom, and Veronica.

And to the hardworking Westword Writers (who often understood my poems better than I did); and to the West Thumb Poets for getting back together!

To Mike, Jim Cunningham, Ed Hill, and other friends of Andy's who helped him countless times.

To Nurse Tracy, Nurse Brenda, and Echo who oversaw Andy's care.

And to Ann Hicks and Barbara Gose, who each brought food.

Thank you with all my heart.

NOTES

Page 5: "CAGED": In the mid-to-late 1970s, Andy was Director of the Navajo County Library System in Arizona, serving the communities of Hopi, Navajo, White Mountain Apache, and Holbrook in person, as well as its Winslow headquarters. He wrote, received, and in some manner oversaw the large grant to remodel that library with wheelchair accommodations. It would be two decades before he himself would need such access.

Page 6: "STEP INTO A GEODE": Andy had a beautiful singing voice, played a cornet, and, I believe, took every music course except band (even Master's-level classes as an undergrad) offered at Northern Arizona University, Flagstaff. He sang in the Shrine of the Ages choir in the Easter Sunrise Service at the South Rim of the Grand Canyon.

Page 22: "WHAT FATE MADE US MOVE TO STATES BURNING ASH": In addition to writing book reviews, Andy had an article, "The Railroad Watch," published in *American Heritage* along with a photo of his Hampden Rail-Way watch. His short story "The Lost Pen of Percival Lowell (From the Fountain Pen of Andy Deering)" won the first Pentrace writing competition and is still online.

Page 41: "I GOT MY HEAD IN FRONT OF THE TIGER": Andy was drawn to animals and felt their specialness and fragility – particularly the rhinoceros, which seemed the first animal whose decline brought international attention to their plight.

Page 60: "I WRITE THE MOON'S MAD FUMBLE": Andy loved meadowlarks. Each spring he would offer $5 to the first one of us (me, our son, or himself) to see one.

A native New Englander, Carol L. Deering has spent most of her life in Wyoming. She has twice been awarded the Wyoming Arts Council Poetry Fellowship (judge Rebecca Foust, 2015; and judge Agha Shahid Ali, 1999). She has twice won the Pierrot Award from Arts in Action. And she has won first place twice in Wyoming Writers, Inc., Free-Verse contests.

She was granted a writing residency at Devils Tower, through a National Park Service competition juried by the Bear Lodge Writers, of Sundance. She worked with the Wyoming Dept. of Education to pull together a successful program, Reading of Writers for Teachers of Writing. She is a founding member of West Thumb Poets, and of Westword Writers.

Carol holds a B.A. in English from Springfield College, and an M.A. in Librarianship & Information Management from the University of Denver. She worked at Central Wyoming College Library for 25 years, the last 12 as Director of Library Services. Her poems appear online, in traditional journals and anthologies, and in her first book, *Havoc & Solace: Poems from the Inland West* (Sastrugi Press, 2018).

Havoc and Solace

Experience the poetry of America's Inland West from an award-winning poet. Venture through the joy, solitude, and sunrise of a thought-provoking author.
www.sastrugipress.com/books/havoc-and-solace/

A Small Pile of Feathers by Gerry Spence

Spence takes them on an emotional journey that connects, calms, and inspires readers. Spence gives hope to those lost in the winter storms of life.

https://www.sastrugipress.com/books/small-pile-feathers/

Is It True by Eugene Gagliano

Is It True? is a delightful collection of children's humorous poetry that children will want to read over and over.

www.sastrugipress.com/crystal-reef-press/is-it-true/

Voices at Twilight by Lori Howe, Ph.D.

Lori Howe invites the reader into the in-between world of past and present in this collection of poems, historical essays, and photographs, all as hauntingly beautiful and austere as the Wyoming landscape they portray.

www.sastrugipress.com/books/voices-at-twilight/

What Did You Say by Eugene Gagliano

Children often misinterpret sayings that adults use and this book helps foster a discussion about them.

www.sastrugipress.com/crystal-reef-press/what-did-you-say/

50 Florida Wildlife Hotspots by Moose Henderson Ph.D.

This is a definitive guide to finding where to photograph wildlife in Florida. Follow the guidance of a professional wildlife photographer as he takes you to some of the best places to see wildlife in the Sunshine State.

www.sastrugipress.com/books/50-florida-wildlife-hotspots/

Antarctic Tears by Aaron Linsdau

Experience the honest story of solo polar exploration. This inspirational true book will make readers both cheer and cry. Coughing up blood and fighting skin-freezing temperatures were only a few of the perils Aaron Linsdau faced.

www.sastrugipress.com/books/antarctic-tears/

Blood Justice by Tim W. James

Two brothers, one a preacher's son, the other an adopted would-be slave, set out in opposite directions to avenge their family's murder only to cross paths in pursuit of the killer.

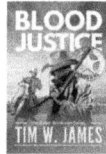

www.sastrugipress.com/iron-spike-press/blood-justice/

Shake Yourself Free by Bob Millsap

Learn how to overcome difficult encounters with misfortune, tragedy, and loss. Emotional recovery is a journey requiring a mindset shift. Get this book now and take control of your life.

www.sastrugipress.com/books/shake-yourself-free/

The Burqa Cave by Dean Petersen

Still haunted by Iraq, Tim Ross finds solace teaching high school in Wyoming. That is, until freshman David Jenkins reveals the murder of a lost local girl. Will Tim be able to overcome his demons to stop the murderer?
www.sastrugipress.com/books/the-burqa-cave/

The Diary of a Dude Wrangler by Struthers Burt

The dude ranch world of Struthers Burt was a romantic destination in the early twentieth century. He made Jackson Hole a tourist destination. These ranches were and still are popular destinations. Experience the origins of the modern old west.
www.sastrugipress.com/books/diary-of-a-dude-wrangler/

The Most Crucial Knots to Know by Aaron Linsdau

Knot tying is a skill everyone can use in daily life. This book shows how to tie over 40 of the most practical knots for virtually any situation. This guide will equip readers with skills that are useful, fun to learn, and will make you look like a confident pro.
www.sastrugipress.com/books/the-most-crucial-knots-to-know/

Use your smart device to scan the QR codes to visit website links.

Visit Sastrugi Press on the web at www.sastrugipress.com to purchase the above titles in bulk. They are also available from your local bookstore or online retailers in print, e-book, or audiobook form. Thank you for choosing Sastrugi Press.

www.sastrugipress.com
"Turn the Page Loose"

Pride and Prejudice by Jane Austen
Follow the story of a family with daughters who struggle to find themselves as they grow up.
www.sastrugipress.com/classics/pride-and-prejudice/

Jane Eyre by Charlotte Brontë
Follow the journey of a young orphan girl as she seeks to find her place in the world and discovers the transformative power of love and the importance of staying true to oneself.
www.sastrugipress.com/classics/jane-eyre/

Robinson Crusoe by Daniel Defoe
A man discovers he is the only survivor of a shipwreck on a deserted island and fights for survival against all odds.
www.sastrugipress.com/classics/robinson-crusoe/

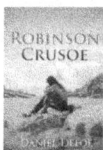

Oliver Twist by Charles Dickens
Charles Dickens's unromantic description of the industrial age of Britain gives insight into the cruelties born by children.
www.sastrugipress.com/classics/oliver-twist/

Discover other Sastrugi Press large print books here:
www.sastrugipress.com/large-print-classics/

www.ingramcontent.com/pod-product-compliance
Lightning Source LLC
LaVergne TN
LVHW091229080426
835509LV00009B/1218